Stories of the Buddha's Past Lives

The Rakshasa Ghost and the Bhikshu

佛陀過去生的故事

羅剎鬼與比丘

Ghost and the Bhikshu
Stories of the Buddha's Past Lives

佛陀過去生的故事

羅剎鬼與比丘

Buddha's Wisdom I

羅刹鬼與比丘
The Rakshasa Ghost and the Bhikshu

宣化上人主講
by the Venerable Master Hsuan Hua

©2005   Dharma Realm Buddhist Association
         Buddhist Text Translation Society
         Dharma Realm Buddhist University

Translated and published by Buddhist Text Translation Society
1777 Murchison Drive, Burlingame, CA94010-4504

First bilingual Chinese/English edition 2005

10 09 08 07 06 05   10 9 8 7 6 5 4 3 2 1
ISBN 986-7328-00-0

Illustrations by: Bodhi Shr, Alicia Yeh
Printed in Taiwan, R.O.C.

Addresses of the Dharma Realm Buddhist Association branches are listed at the back of this book.

Ghost and the Bhikshu
Stories of the Buddha's Past Lives

Contents 目錄

- 2/ 給父母的話
    ——與佛陀的智慧相遇
    Words for parents:
    "Meet with Buddha's Wisdom"

- 8/ 給小讀者的話
    ——智慧的小園丁
    Words for younger readers:
    "A Little Gardener of Wisdom"

- 14/ 佛陀過去生的故事
    Stories of the Buddha's Past Lives

    - 18/ 鹿野苑
        The Deer Park

    - 48/ 大龜王
        The Great Turtle King

    - 70/ 六牙象王
        The Six-tusked Elephant King

    - 90/ 羅剎鬼與比丘
        The Rakshasa Ghost and
        the Bhikshu

    - 110/ 布髮掩泥
        Hair That Covered Mud

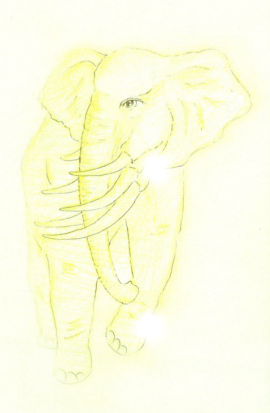

給父母的話：與佛陀的智慧相遇

慧覺/文

by Hui-Jiao

十五歲的小婕，有一天
當她發現愛因斯坦也是一位素食者時，
她興奮地對媽媽說：
「愛因斯坦和我一樣，也是吃素的耶！」
從此有了這位世紀科學家的加入，
小婕和同學聚餐時，再也不會覺得尷尬，
甚至還挺自豪自己的選擇。

One day, fifteen-year old Jessie

discovered that Albert Einstein was also a vegetarian.

She excitedly told her mother,

"Albert Einstein and I are the same. We are both vegetarians!"

After learning of this renowned scientist's eating habits,

Jessie no longer felt embarrassed when eating with her friends,

and was even proud of her choice.

Words for parents: "With Buddha's Wisdom"

的確，孩子的成長需要關心，
需要鼓勵，也需要同儕的認同和歸屬。
父母、師長、同學、公眾人物，
甚至卡通或是小說裏虛擬的人物，
都可以在孩子的學習過程中，
成爲他們崇拜模仿的對象。因此我們
決定出版這套「佛陀的智慧」系列叢書，
幫助孩子認識更多佛陀的行誼，
希望在他們純眞的心靈世界裏，
多一位值得「見賢思齊」的好榜樣。

Indeed, while growing up, children need care, encouragement from parents, and a sense of belonging and recognition from their peers.

Parents, teachers, classmates, leaders in society, even cartoon or fictional characters are all possible role models and idols for children during their development. Therefore, we are publishing this Buddha's Wisdom series, with the hope that today's youth can learn more during their formative years about the Buddha's virtue and about his conduct and deeds.

This series will provide our youth
with one more worthy role model to learn from and admire.

給父母的話：
與佛陀的智慧相遇
"Meet

另外一個促成「佛陀的智慧」出版的因緣，
係為了實踐宣公上人生前的
三大弘願：弘法、譯經和教育。
因此書中所收錄的故事，
除了〈大龜王〉鑒於孩子的閱讀程度，
而由編者撰文補入外，
其餘的均來自宣公上人親自的講述。
當年上人用這些故事，
來幫助弟子們明白佛法的精神，
現在我們配合著故事的內容，
繪出一幅幅生動的插畫，
希望當文字翻譯成圖畫後，
能讓甚深微妙的佛法，
與孩子的世界更接近。

Words for parents: "With Buddha's Wisdom"

Moreover, publishing the Buddha's Wisdom series
also helps fulfill the Venerable Master's three great vows.
The Master wanted to spread the Buddha's teachings,
sponsor the translation of the Buddha's sutras,
and do his utmost to provide good education for students.
Among the stories in this book,
The Great Turtle King has been rewritten in language
that is suitable for children.
However, the rest of the stories are gathered
from the Venerable Master's commentaries.
The Venerable Master told these stories to help his disciples
understand the spirit of the Buddha's teaching.
Now, we are bringing these stories to life with attractive illustrations,
hoping that through colorful pictures,
we can draw children closer to the profound and wonderful Dharma,
the teachings of the Buddha.

給父母的話：
與佛陀的智慧相遇

"Meet

本系列首先推出的是《羅剎鬼與比丘》，
介紹釋迦牟尼佛在過去生修行的故事。
目的是希望孩子們從故事中，
體會菩薩慈悲喜捨的精神，
同時也明白「因地修行」的因果道理。
再繼《羅剎鬼與比丘》之後，
我們預計推出的下一本童畫書，是介紹
佛陀今生捨棄王位、出家修道，
以及最後在尼連河畔開悟的種種經過，
該書將命名為《真正的覺者》。

The first book in this series, *The Rakshasa Ghost and the Bhikshu*, introduces stories of Shakyamuni Buddha's cultivation in past lives, when he was a Bodhisattva.

The purpose is to teach children about the Bodhisattvas' kindness, compassion, joy and giving. At the same time,

Words for parents: "With Buddha's Wisdom"

the tales told in this book will help children understand cause and effect.
What the Buddha did in the past created causes
that brought on later effects. Following *The Rakshasa Ghost and the Bhikshu*
is the second book titled *The Truly Awakened One*.
This book tells the story of how the Buddha realized Buddhahood.
We find out about the Buddha's decision to give up the throne,
leave the home life and cultivate the Way,
his enlightenment on the banks of the Neranjara River and other events.

現在就邀請您和孩子，
與佛陀這位真正的覺者相遇，
一同漫遊在佛法浩瀚的覺海裏，
開拓我們生命的視野，
鑿出自性中「人人本具，個個不無」
的智慧明珠！

We encourage you to accompany your child on a journey to meet
the truly Awakened One and to submerge yourself in the sea of awakening.
May you and your children share in opening your eyes to life
and in rediscovering the self-nature inherent in us all.
It is the true pearl of wisdom!

給小讀者的話：智慧的小園丁
Words for "A Little...

小豆芽/文

By Little Beansprout

小朋友，你種過植物嗎？回想一下，
如果希望植物長得好，你必須怎麼做？
是不是要讓它每天曬曬太陽，
呼吸點新鮮空氣，
偶爾還要給它喝一點水？
如果你能和它講講話，
它還會長得更好哩！這就對了，
不只我們是這樣，佛陀也是這樣。

Young friends, have you ever planted any plants before?

If you want the plants to grow nicely, what do you have to do?

Plants need sunlight everyday. They like fresh air,

and they must have water to drink once in a while.

If you to talk to them, they will grow even better.

That's right!

We are caregivers for the plants we grow.

The Buddha is a caregiver, too.

Younger readers: "Gardener of Wisdom"

我們每個人的心，
就像一塊肥沃的田，
裏面藏著許多善良和智慧的種子。
為了令這些種子能夠發芽、茁壯，
佛陀放棄王子的榮華富貴，
離開王宮，出家修行。

Our mind is like a piece of fertile soil in which
many seeds of goodness and wisdom are planted.
In order to help these seeds sprout and become strong,
the Buddha renounced the luxury and wealth
he would have inherited.
Instead, he left his home in the palace
and went forth to cultivate the Way.

給小讀者的話：
智慧的小園丁
Words for "A Little

他思考並且嘗試種種的方法，
細心、耐心地照顧著它們，
直到最後在雪山開悟，
得到最圓滿的智慧。
所以我們稱佛陀為「真正的覺者」，
意思就是一位有真正智慧的人，
因為他的智慧種子，
已經成功地長成了大樹。

The Buddha first experimented with

his own seeds of goodness and wisdom.

He tried various methods to

patiently and prudently cultivate those sprouts.

When at last he became enlightened on Snow Mountain,

his seeds ripened into supreme and perfect wisdom.

He became a Buddha, an Awakened One.

His title means he perfected his own true wisdom.

His seeds of wisdom grew into a mighty tree.

Younger readers: "Gardener of Wisdom"

不僅在今生是這樣的努力認真，
其實佛陀在他過去無數的生命裏，
就已經不斷的栽培這些種子。
所以這本《羅剎鬼與比丘》，
描述的就是
佛陀在過去生修行的故事。

Not only had the Buddha taken good care
of his seeds in that life, he had been tending
and nurturing those seeds for a long time,
in many previous lives.
The Rakshasa Ghost and the Bhikshu tells us about
what the Buddha did before.

給小讀者的話：
智慧的小園丁
Words for "A Little

在我們心田的這些種子，
和任何植物的種子一樣，
也需要像陽光、空氣和水的滋潤
才能吐出小芽，然後成長茁壯。
那麼到底什麼是它需要的養份呢？
別急著回答，只要你翻開這本書，
一頁一頁讀下去，你就知道答案了！

The seeds in the field of our mind are like the seeds

we plant in the ground.

Our seeds of goodness and wisdom

also need sun, air, and water for nourishment.

Then they can germinate and become robust.

What kind of fertilizer should we use?

Ah! Save that question for now.

Just keep reading this book page by page,

and you will discover many answers all by yourself!

"Younger readers: Gardener of Wisdom"

現在讓我們一起向佛陀看齊,
學做一個智慧的小園丁,
灌溉栽培這些善良的種子,
讓它們也成為一棵豐碩的大樹。
小朋友, 準備好了嗎?
故事馬上開始囉!

Now, let us follow the Buddha's lead

and learn how we can each be a little gardener of wisdom.

Remember to be an attentive caregiver

for your own seeds of goodness

so that one day they will ripen.

Then, like the Buddha,

we will each become a grand and flourishing tree.

Young friends, are you ready?

The adventure will begin now!

Stories of the Buddha's

佛陀過去生的故事

Past Lives

我們都知道
釋迦牟尼佛出生在印度，
本來是一位王子，
後來出家，修行成佛。

可是事實上，
佛陀不是只有這一次來到這個世界，
他已經以各種面目
降生到這個世界好多好多次了。
在這麼多生中，
佛陀不斷地修習種種的行門，
累積無數的福德，
奠定了未來成佛的基礎，
這就叫「因地修行」。
現在讓我們來聽聽
佛陀在因地修行的本生故事吧！

History shows us that Shakyamuni Buddha
was born as a prince in India.
Later, he left home and became a Buddha. But in reality,
the Buddha did not come only once to this Earth.
He came many, many times
in different forms and with different faces.
In all those many lives,
he continuously practiced and cultivated the Way.
Courageously, he accumulated measureless merit,
and secured the future foundations for attaining Buddhahood.
This is called "cultivation at the level of planting causes."
Now, let us listen to the original story of the Buddha cultivating
at the level of planting causes.

鹿野苑
The Deer Park

你是一隻人頭鹿
而我卻是一個鹿頭人
You have the head of a human,
while I have the head of a deer.

從前有座美麗的大園子，
園子裏面長滿了鮮艷奪目的花朵，
濃密的大樹蔭覆著綠茵般的草地，
景色非常宜人。若非發生一件可悲的事，
這座大園子可說是兩大鹿群的美妙家園。

A long time ago, in a beautiful park,
attractive, brightly colored flowers flourished.
Dense trees cast a cool shade over
lush, green grass. It was a charming place.
If a dreadful event did not occur,
this grand park could be said
to be the pleasant home of two herds of deer.

原來這個國家的國王
不但是個肉食者，而且
還特別喜愛吃鹿肉。
每天，他都到園子
裏捕殺鹿來吃。
雖然國王愛吃鹿肉，
但是他每天最多只能吃半隻；
而他帶去打獵的人很多，
一打就不知道打死多少鹿。
於是被殺的鹿，
遠超過國王所需要的，
結果很多的鹿就白白犧牲了。

There was a human King in the country

in which the Deer Park was situated.

He loved to eat meat, but not just any type of meat.

He particularly loved to eat venison.

Everyday he would go to the Deer Park to hunt deer.

Although the King loved venison,

he could only eat half a deer per day.

Yet he took with him a whole group of hunters.

With each chase, they killed numerous deer,

which was more than enough for the King.

As a result, many deer were sacrificed needlessly.

這兩群鹿各有
一隻俊俏
又強壯的雄鹿
做為牠們的領袖；
這兩隻鹿王
一隻是白的，
一隻是黑的，
於是
兩隻鹿王就開會，
開什麼會呢？

Each of the herds of deer was led
by a regal and strong buck.
One deer king was white colored,
and the other was black.
These two deer king
had a meeting between themselves.
What was the meeting about?

白鹿王說：

「我們現在應該救我們眷屬的生命，
不要讓國王把我們都殺死了，
怎麼救法呢？
我們到國王那兒去請願，
要求他不要再來殺鹿。
但是我們答應國王，
每天由兩個鹿群，輪流送
一隻鹿給國王做飲食。
這樣我們的眷屬
就不會斷滅，
國王也天天有
新鮮的鹿肉吃了。
我相信國王
會答應我們的請求，
因為他如果天天捕殺
這麼多鹿的話，
鹿很快就會絕種了，
國王也就沒鹿肉吃了。」
黑鹿王一聽，說：
「好啊！
我們就去請願！」

White Deer King said,

"We should save the lives of our family and friends.

We shouldn't let the King kill us all.

How should we save ourselves?

We should go before the King with our request

that he won't hunt us anymore."

But we shall tell the King that every day

we will take turns sending a deer

from our own herds as the King's food.

This way, our family and friends will not all perish

and the King will also have fresh venison daily.

I think the King will agree to our request

because if he continues to kill us off at such a rate,

the deer will perish, and he will run out of venison to eat."

After hearing this, Black Deer King said,

"Right! Let's go make that request right now."

於是兩隻鹿王就到國王那兒去請願。
一到國王的宮殿門口,
守門的衛兵,
看見來了兩隻大鹿,
就拿起茅槍要刺牠們,
兩隻大鹿說:
「你不要殺我們,
我們今天來,是要見國王,
我們想向國王請願。」
這衛兵一聽,鹿會說人話?
覺得很奇怪,於是就報告國王
說有兩隻會說人話的鹿來了。
國王聽說鹿會說人話,也很驚奇,
就准許牠們進來請願。

Thus,
the two deer kings went to the King's palace
to present their petition.
The gatekeeper of the palace saw the two deer
and raised his spear to strike them.
The two deer kings said,
"Don't strike us.
We came today to see the King.
We would like to talk to him."
When the guard heard them, he was shocked.
He wondered,
"How can deer speak human language?"
He reported to the King
that two talking deer had
come to see him.
The King was also amazed
that deer could speak.
So he allowed the two deer
to come see him.

本來國王看到兩隻鹿會說人話，
已經很奇怪了，
再一聽牠們的請願，
覺得很合理，
就批准了，說：
「可以的！
你們每天送一隻鹿來。」
就這樣，
每天都送一隻鹿來給國王吃，
國王天天吃新鮮鹿肉，覺得很美味。

The king was awed by the talking deer.

He heard their request and felt that it was reasonable.

He agreed and said, "Yes! Every day send a deer to me."

So it was, each day a deer was sent to the king to eat.

Every day the King had fresh venison

and found it delicious.

有一天,
　白鹿王親身入宮覲見國王,
　　國王問他:
「你今天怎麼到這裏來了?」
「我到這裏來,
　　是為了供你今天食用。」

One day, White Deer King himself came to the King.

The King asked, "What brings you here today?"

"I came here today to offer you your food."

國王大吃一驚，就說：
「你是鹿王，怎麼可以來進貢？
難道你的鹿眷屬、你的子孫都沒有了嗎？」
「我的眷屬不但有，而且一天比一天增加，
我和黑鹿王各管五百頭鹿，
一天只送一頭鹿給國王您食用，
其餘的母鹿生出很多小鹿，
所以現在我們的眷屬繁殖了幾倍，
比以前多得多。
不過現在有一個因緣，所以我親自來進貢。」
「什麼緣故？」

The King was taken aback, and said,

"You are a deer king. How can you be the offering?

Is it that you have no more relatives or descendents left?"

"Not only does my herd have many, our numbers grow by the day.

My herd has five hundred deer

and Black Deer King's herd also has five hundred deer.

Each day we send you only one deer to eat.

The does give birth to many fawns.

That is why our population not only has recovered,

but has multiplied many times over.

But right now we have a problem,

so I have personally come to offer myself as your food."

"What is the problem?"

「今天本來是輪到
一隻黑鹿王群中的母鹿,
來獻給您吃。
但是這隻母鹿,
再過一兩天就要生小鹿了,
所以就向黑鹿王哀求說:
『我不在乎輪到我去死,
但希望等到鹿兒出世後才去。
如果今天我被殺,
腹中的鹿兒也要死了。
您可以找另外一隻代替我去嗎?
當我生了鹿兒後,
我會很願意去的。』

"Originally, today was the turn of a doe

in Black Deer King's herd to be presented for your meal.

But this doe is about to give birth in a day or two.

So she went to the Black Deer King to plead,

'I'm not afraid of dying, but I hope I can give birth to my fawn before I go.

If I am killed today, the fawn in my womb will die too.

Can you please find someone else to take my place until then?

Once I give birth, I will be willing to go.'"

但是黑鹿王不准調換,
這隻母鹿就淚汪汪地來同我商量,
想在我這邊調換。

"But the Black Deer King did not allow the exchange.
So the doe came to me with tears in her eyes.
She wanted to see if any deer in my herd would
be willing to make the exchange.

但是我一想,
我這邊雖然有五百隻鹿,
但沒有輪到誰,
誰都不願先來送死。
於是我就叫母鹿
住在我的鹿群裏待產,
自己親身來替她死。」

"But I knew that even though
there are five hundred members in my herd,
none would like to die a day earlier than their turn.
So I told the doe to stay in my herd while
I, myself, took her place."

這個國王一聽,
大受感動,
啊! 有這麼奇怪的事情!
因為白鹿王是個領袖,
就算再過好多年,
牠都可以輕而易舉地
避免被殺的;
而現在竟然願意為一隻
並非在牠管轄之下的母鹿,
犧牲自己的性命!

The King, upon hearing this, was very touched.
What unusual circumstances!
Because White Deer King was the leader,
he could live many years and easily avoid death.
But now, he was willing to sacrifice his own life for a doe
that was not even in his herd.

國王很慚愧，
原來鹿也是眾生之一，
我為什麼天天要吃鹿肉呢？
於是就說：
「汝為鹿頭人，我為人頭鹿，
從今以後，誓不食肉。」
這是說，
你雖然長著一個鹿的頭，
但是你的心非常仁慈，
比人的心還好。
而我雖然長著一個人的頭，
但是我的心不如鹿的心。
從今天之後，
什麼肉我都不吃了。

The King felt remorseful. "Even deer cherish their lives.
Why do I want to eat venison every day?" he thought.
So he said, "You are a human with a deer's head,
while I am a deer with a human head.
You have a benevolent heart that is kinder than a human's.
Although I have the head of a human,
my heart is no better than a deer's.
From this day on,
I will eat no more meat of any kind."

這是白鹿王把國王感動得吃齋了！
所以園子中的兩群鹿
便在那兒大量地繁殖了；
因為有許多鹿，
在那兒快樂自由的生活著，
所以就被稱為鹿野苑，又叫鹿園，
還有一個特別名字叫仙苑。

This is how White Deer King

moved the King to become a vegetarian.

And so the two herds of deer

in that park greatly multiplied.

Because of the great number of deer

living a carefree existence in that park,

the park became known as

Wild Deer Park or Deer Park.

It is also called Park of the Immortals.

為什麼叫仙苑？
因為這個地方，風景幽美，
風水也好，有很多仙人，
都住在這兒修道的緣故。
而釋迦牟尼佛成佛了以後，
也是先到鹿野苑度五比丘。

Why is it called Park of the Immortals?
Because the view is beautiful,
the geomancy is favorable,
and many holy ones come here to cultivate.
After Shakyamuni Buddha attained Buddhahood,
he came to this place to enlighten the five Bhikshus.

故事到此就結束了。
不過，還有一件事要特別提一提，
那隻白鹿王，
就是釋迦牟尼佛的前生，
他在多生多劫以前，行菩薩道，
做一隻仁慈的鹿王，來教化眾生。
而黑鹿王呢？
就是提婆達多的前生，
也就是佛陀今生的堂弟。
他常常和佛作對，在許多世中，
他們常常有因緣相遇在一起。

The story ends here.

But we must mention that White Deer King

was a past incarnation of Shakyamuni Buddha.

For many lifetimes and eons,

he walked the Bodhisattva Path.

By being a kind-hearted deer king,

he enlightened many living creatures.

And who was Black Deer King?

He was a past incarnation of Devadatta,

who was the Buddha's cousin.

He often opposed the Buddha.

They met often in different lives.

智慧出爐！
Your wisdom has surfaced!

請回答下列問題：
Let's see if you can answer the following questions:

- 小朋友，請畫一幅本故事中鹿野苑的景像。
  Please draw a picture of
  the scenery from the story of the Deer Park.

- 兩隻鹿王怎麼保護牠們的眷屬？
  How did the two deer kings save their relatives and friends?

- 白鹿王怎麼感化國王吃齋？
  How did White Deer King
  persuade the King to become a vegetarian?

- 白鹿王是誰的前生呢？
  Who was White Deer King the past incarnation of?

The Great Turtle King 大龜王

人們誤以為這是
沙灘上的一片土地
就開始在牠的背上
建立起自己的家園……

Mistaking him for a piece of sandy land,
people started building their homes
upon his back...

很久很久以前，
在深深的藍海裏，
有一隻
非常非常巨大的海龜，
牠既仁慈又英明，
於是魚鱉蝦蟹等水族，
就選牠為海中之王。
在牠的領導下，
大家和和樂樂地相處在一起，
日子過得快樂極了！

A long, long time ago,

in the deep blue sea,

lived a gigantic sea turtle.

He was very kind and wise.

Thus,

all the fish, turtles, shrimps, crabs,

and creatures of the sea chose him as their king.

Under his rule,

everyone lived together harmoniously and happily.

Every day was filled with joy.

有一天,
大龜王爬到沙灘上曬太陽,
在陽光和煦地照耀下,
哇!好舒服喔!
所以不知不覺地睡著了。
牠睡得很沉很沉……
很久很久……
於是──

One day,

the Great Turtle King crawled to

the shore to bask in the sun.

The earth was warm and cozy

beneath the radiant sun.

Ah! How comfortable!

And so, without knowing, he fell fast asleep.

He slept very, very deeply,

and for a very, very long time.

Then...

風沙覆蓋了牠，
雨水流進龜殼的縫隙，
形成了河流，
甚至花草樹木也長出來了！
因為牠的身體是如此地龐大，
人們誤以為
這是沙灘上的一片土地，
絲毫也察覺不到這是「龜背」！
就開始在牠背上，
建立起他們的家園。
漸漸地，
移居到龜背上的人越來越多，
他們不但蓋上了房子，
還開設商店，鋪了馬路，
造了一座大城市！
人們和動物在龜背上行走，
車輛頻頻在上面來回穿梭，
可是，
大龜王竟然還在沉睡中！

The wind blew sand over him and slowly covered him.

The rain flowed down the grooves of his shell, forming streams and rivers.

Even flowers, grass, trees, and shrubs started sprouting on his back.

His body was so immense that people mistook him for a piece of land.

No one had the slightest idea that it was a turtle's back.

Thus, they started building their community on his back.

Gradually, more and more people moved there.

They not only built their homes there,

they opened stores and shops, paved roads,

and constructed a great city.

Both people and animals treaded upon his back.

Carts busily commuted on it, back and forth, to and fro.

But the Great Turtle King slumbered on!

地震啦

然而，
　　城市重重地
　　　　壓在大龜王的背上，
人們的吵雜聲
　　如捶鼓般
　　　　振動牠的耳朵；
他們所燃的火，
　　更是無情地
　　　　燒透了牠的殼！
有一天，
　　大龜王終於從喧雜和燒灼的
　　痛苦中醒來了！
　　　　牠渾身不自在，
　　　　　　急忙轉身回到海裏去，
想讓浪花冷卻熱騰騰的身體。

But the great city

    weighed heavily up on the turtle's back.

        The noise of the people pounded against

            his ears like the beating of drums.

                The fires they made burned mercilessly

                    through his shell.

One day,

    due to the agony of the noisy clamoring

        and scorching heat,

            he finally awoke!

Feeling uncomfortable all over,

    he quickly turned around

        to head back to the sea,

            hoping the waves would cool

                his feverish body.

這時，
　　牠聽到「地震！地震！」的狂叫聲，
　　　又聽到「洪水！洪水！」的哭喊聲
——大龜王才知道，
　　原來人們已經在牠的背上
　　　建立了家園，
　　　　在那兒生活著。
牠知道如果移動身體，
　　不但會嚇壞他們，
　　　並且還會傷害到他們；
為了不給人們
　　帶來煩惱和痛苦，
　　　只好小心的
　　　　爬回海灘上，
默默地忍受著。

Then he heard people screaming in panic,
"Earthquake! Earthquake!"
Others cried, "Flood! Flood!"
He finally realized that people had built homes
on his back and settled there.
He knew that if he moved his body,
he would frighten and injure them.
In order to alleviate their worry and suffering,
he carefully crawled back onto shore
and silently endured the pain.

一天、兩天……，
　一年、兩年……，
　　一百年、兩百年……又過去了，
　　　大龜王每天默默忍受
　　　　火燒、耳鳴、重壓的痛苦。
可是牠的痛苦、
　牠的犧牲、牠的淚水，
　　卻沒有人知道。

One day, two days,
　one year, two years,
　　one hundred years,
　　　two hundred years,
　　　　the time passed.
Every day the Great Turtle King
　silently endured the blazing fires,
　　the ringing in his ears, and the oppressive pain.
　　　But nobody knew of his misery,
　　　　his sacrifice, and the tears he shed.

日子一天一天地過去，
背上的壓力與熱焰，
也越來越厲害。
有一天，
牠實在痛苦得忍不住了，
牠決定必須回到海裏。
於是稍微移動一下，
想散發身上的熱氣。
這時住在背上的居民
立刻騷動起來：
「地震呀！
　　地震呀！」
大龜王聽到他們
驚慌地大叫，
便抬起頭
對他們說：
「不用怕，
　我不會傷害你們的。
　　你們看，我是一隻海龜！
　　　而你們卻在我的背上建立家園！
　　　　現在我必須要回去，
　　　　　否則我會死掉。」

Time passed, day by day.
The pressures and hot flames on his back
grew more and more intense.
One day he truly could not stand the pain anymore,
so he decided to head back to the ocean.
Thus, he moved a bit in hopes of venting out some
of the heat on his body.
At that moment, the people on his back
immediately raised a commotion,
"Earthquake! Earthquake!"
The Great Turtle King
heard their frightened cries.
He then lifted his head and said to them,
"Don't be afraid. I won't hurt you.
Look, I am a sea turtle!
And you have been building
your homes upon my back!
Now I must go back to the sea,
or else I will die."

當人們
　　從海龜王背上爬下來時，
　　　想到大海龜無聲無息地，
　　　　為他們受了這麼久的痛苦，
　　　　　大受感動，
　　　　　　便向大龜王頂禮，
並且發願：
「您真是一位菩薩啊！
　　犧牲自己，
　　　保護我們的生命財產，
　　　　將來您成佛時，
　　請記得回來救度我們。」

While the inhabitants climbed down from the Great Turtle King's back,
they thought back on how he had silently endured
such great pain for their sake.
They were extremely touched
and bowed to the Great Turtle King.
Furthermore, they vowed,
"You really are a Bodhisattva,
sacrificing yourself to protect
our lives and property.
When you attain Buddhahood,
please remember to
come back and save us.

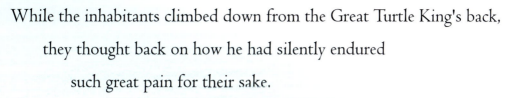

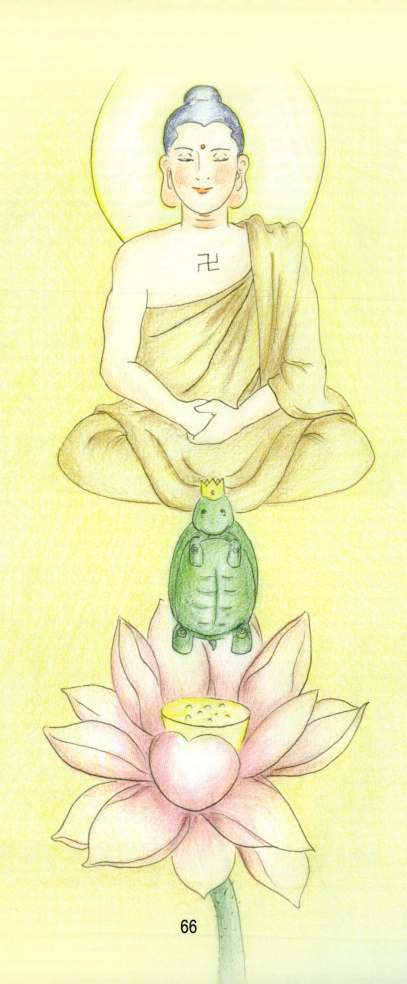

後來， 大龜王果然成佛了──
那就是釋迦牟尼佛。
當時住在龜背上的五百個居民，
便轉生為佛的弟子。
他們受佛的教化後，
都了生脫死， 證得聖果。

Later, the Great Turtle King indeed attained Buddhahood.

He became Shakyamuni Buddha.

Those five hundred inhabitants

who lived on his back were reborn as his disciples.

After the Buddha taught them,

they all were freed from the cycle of birth and death

and eventually attained enlightenment.

智慧出爐！
Your wisdom has surfaced!

請回答下列問題：
Let's see if you can answer the following questions:

● 小朋友，如果你是大龜王，遇到像牠一樣的情況，你會怎麼處理？
If you were the Great Turtle King
and met with the same situation, what would you have done?

● 住在龜背上的人，是哪些人的過去生？
Who did those people who lived on the back
of the giant turtle become in the future?

● 想想看還有哪些動物救人的故事？講出來給你的朋友聽一聽。
Can you think of other stories where animals saved people?
Please share them with your friends.

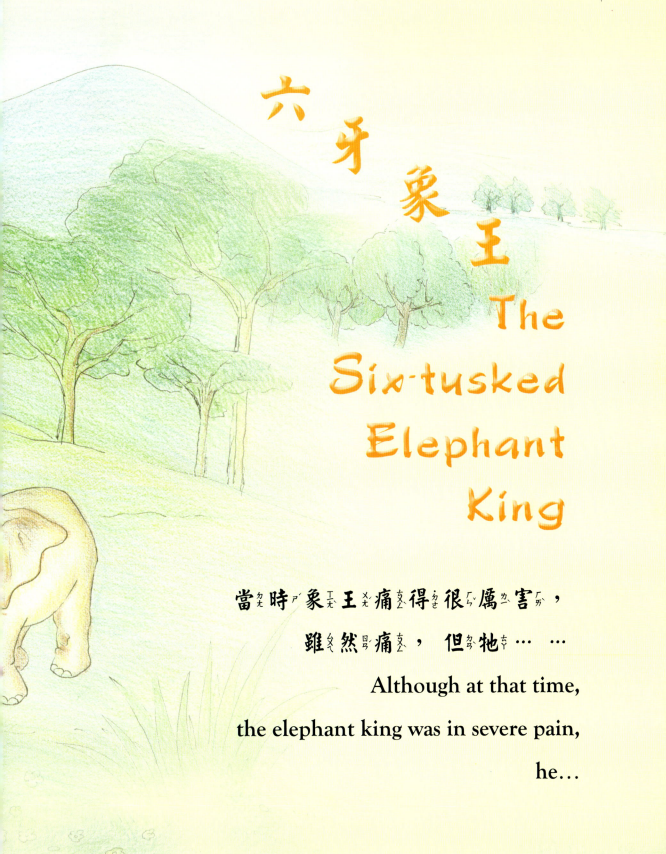

六牙象王
The Six-tusked Elephant King

當時象王痛得很厲害，雖然痛，但牠……

Although at that time, the elephant king was in severe pain, he…

從前在一座茂密的森林裏，
有一隻象王，
領導著一群象
在那裏優游快樂地生活著。
這隻象王
可不是普通的象，
一般象只有兩支象牙，
而牠卻有六支
美麗又潔白的長牙，
不只這樣，最重要的是
牠有一顆既善良又仁慈的心，
所以象群們都非常愛戴牠們的王。

Once upon a time,
in a very dense forest, there lived an elephant king.
He led a herd of elephants in a happy and carefree life.
This elephant was not an ordinary elephant,
for ordinary elephants have only two tusks.
This elephant had six exquisite tusks
that were clean, white, and long.
Besides this, his most important quality was
that he had a very compassionate heart,
and so his herd loved and respected him.

那時
有一個國家的國王，
想得到這隻象王的牙，
於是就派了幾個最貧賤的人，
穿上出家人的袈裟，
拿著毒箭，
慢慢走到象王的身邊。

At that time, the king of the country wanted to
obtain the elephant's six tusks.
The king dispatched a few really poor people.
He told them to disguise themselves in the robes of Bhikshus,
take with them a few poisonous arrows,
and slowly make their way to the elephant king.

母象看見有人穿著袈裟,
手裏拿著弓箭來了,
就趕快去告訴象王,說:
「大王,有一些人想要偷偷地來殺我們,
我們趕快逃避!」
象王說:「這些人穿著比丘的袈裟,
比丘都是沒有惡心的,我們不需要逃避。」
於是就在那兒等著。

The queen elephant saw these people disguised
in the robes of Bhikshus carrying bows and arrows.
She hurried to tell the king, "Oh Mighty King,
there are a few people creeping over here to kill you.
Quick, let us all escape!"
The elephant king said,
"These people wear the robes of Bhikshus.
Bhikshus have no evil intentions.
We don't need to escape."
And so the elephants waited.

結果這幾個人接近象王時，
就用毒箭射中象王的身，
母象不禁大聲悲號，
這時其餘的象一看，都發脾氣了，
想用腳把這幾個人踩死。

As a result,

when the people got close to the elephant king,

they shot him with poisonous arrows.

The queen elephant instinctively called out plaintively.

When the rest of the herd turned around to see what had happened,

they became so angry, they were ready to trample the trespassers.

象王說：「不要把這些人踩死！我問問他們為什麼用箭來射我？」
象王就問這幾個穿比丘袈裟的人：
「你們為什麼要來射我呢？」
「因為我們的國王想要得到你六支象牙，所以命令我們來射你。」

The elephant king stopped them, saying,

"Don't trample them! I'll ask them why they shot me with arrows."

The elephant king then turned to the people disguised

in the robes of Bhikshus and asked, "Why did you shoot me?"

"Our king wants your six tusks, so we were ordered to shoot you."

「那容易！
你們要得到我的牙是很容易的，
我這就給你們。」
於是象王用自己的鼻子，
把牙都拔下來，交給
這幾個人拿回去獻給國王，
並且對象群說：
「我寧願捨棄生命，
也不對眾生起殺心。」
牠又對那幾個人說：
「我現在將身上的白牙
布施給你們，
沒有一點憤怒
也沒有一點捨不得，
唯願以此布施的福德，
種來日成佛的因，
幫助眾生滅除煩惱病苦。」

"That is easy! You can get my tusks very easily.
Let me give them to you now."
And so the elephant king used his own trunk to pull out his tusks.
He handed his tusks to the people to present to their king.
Then he said to his herd, "I'd rather sacrifice my own life
than give rise to the thought of killing any creature."
He turned back to the people and said,
"Now I am going to bequeath to you my tusks,
without wrath and without reluctance.
I only hope that the merit created from this sacrifice
will be the seed planted for Buddhahood in the future,
and it will help all living beings eradicate worry and suffering."

當時
象王痛得很厲害，
雖然痛，
但牠忍著。因為
這是菩薩示現象身，
來教化所有的象，
所以叫六牙象王菩薩。
這位菩薩是誰呢？
就是釋迦牟尼佛
往昔修菩薩行時，
示現的一隻六牙象王菩薩。
佛在因地的時候，
布施牙齒、頭目腦髓給一切眾生，
你看看這是他現一隻象的身，
布施牙齒給國王。

Although at that time,
the elephant king was in severe pain,
he endured it.
In reality,
he was a bodhisattva taking on the
form of an elephant to enlighten all the elephants,
so we call him the Six-tusked Elephant King Bodhisattva.
Who was this Bodhisattva?
It was Shakyamuni Buddha who took on the
form of the Six-Tusked Elephant King
when he was cultivating
the Bodhisattva Path in the past.
When the Buddha was performing
these meritorious deeds through countless lifetimes,
he not only sacrificed his teeth,
but also his head, eyes, brain,
and marrow to all living beings.
Look at how he took on the form of an elephant
and sacrificed his tusks to the king.

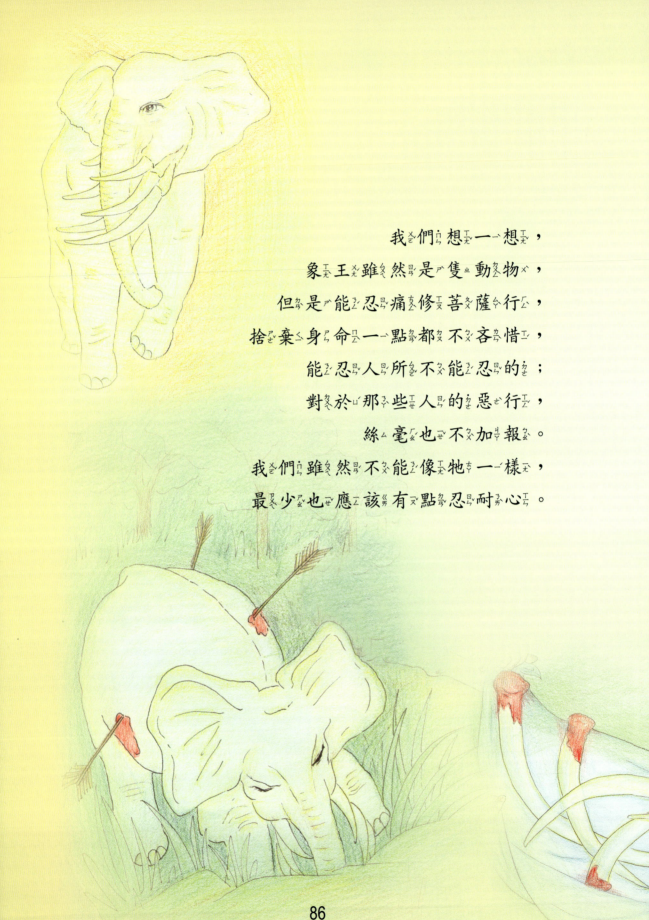

我們想一想，
象王雖然是隻動物，
但是能忍痛修菩薩行，
捨棄身命一點都不吝惜，
能忍人所不能忍的；
對於那些人的惡行，
絲毫也不加報。
我們雖然不能像牠一樣，
最少也應該有點忍耐心。

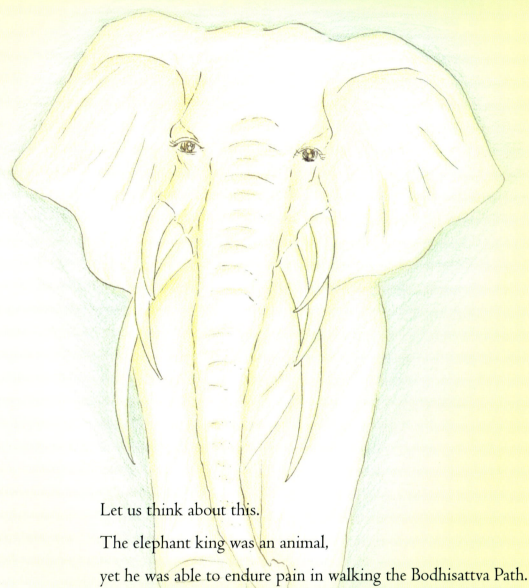

Let us think about this.

The elephant king was an animal,

yet he was able to endure pain in walking the Bodhisattva Path.

He was able to sacrifice his life without a bit of selfishness.

He could endure what others could not endure.

He did not harbor the slightest thought of revenge toward

those people with evil intentions.

Even though we cannot be exactly like the elephant king,

we should at least have more fortitude and patience.

智慧出爐！
Your wisdom has surfaced!

請回答下列問題：

Let's see if you can answer the following questions:

● 小朋友，這幾個穿比丘袈裟的人，為什麼要來射殺六牙象王呢？

Why did those people disguised in the robes of Bhikshus want to shoot Six-tusked Elephant King?

● 六牙象王把自己最珍貴的象牙布施給了國王，你曾有過布施的經驗嗎？

Six-tusked Elephant King sacrificed his most precious tusks to the king. Have you ever given anything away?

● 你送給別人的東西，是你喜歡的東西？還是不喜歡的東西？

When you give things to others, do you chose things you like or things you don't like?

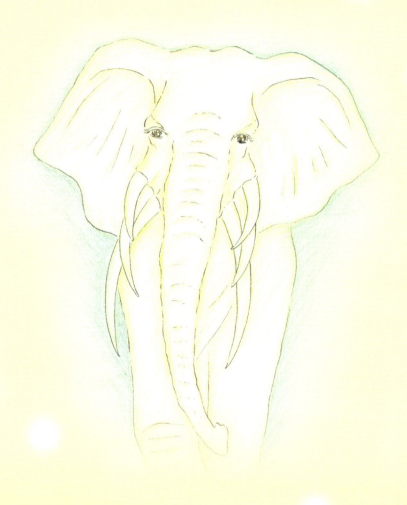

羅剎鬼與比丘
The Rakshasa Ghost and the Bhikshu

你想多聽聞一些佛法嗎？
可是，我現在很餓，
必須先吃點東西……

Do you want to hear more Buddhadharma?
But then again, I'm getting a bit hungry.
I must eat something first....

很久久很久以前，
釋迦牟尼佛有一生
是一位比丘（就是出家的和尚）。
一天，
這位比丘遇到一個吃人的羅剎鬼；
當這位比丘經過他的身旁時，
聽見他說了兩句偈頌：

　　　　諸行無常，　是生滅法

一聽到這兩句偈，
這位比丘非常地高興。

A long, long time ago,
Shakyamuni Buddha was a Bhikshu (which is a monk who has left home).
One day, this Bhikshu met a *rakshasa* ghost who ate people.
As the Bhikshu walked past him, he heard him say,

　　　"Everything is impermanent.
　　　　Where there is production, there is extinction."

Upon hearing this, the Bhikshu became very happy.

於是他對羅剎鬼說：
「聽到你說的佛法，
使我非常快樂。
但是你的偈頌似乎還沒有說完，
你才說了兩句，還沒有說完呢！
請你快快告訴我後面的偈頌吧！」

He asked the *rakshasa* ghost,

"Hearing you speak the Buddhadharma makes me very happy.

Yet, your verse seems incomplete.

You only spoke two phrases; you didn't finish!

Please hurry and tell me the rest of the verse!"

羅剎鬼用他又大又紅的眼睛
瞪著這位比丘說：
「哦！你想多聽聞一些佛法嗎？
可是，我現在很餓，必須先吃點東西。
如果不吃東西，就沒辦法再說任何佛法了！
而我最喜歡吃的就是人肉，
除非你讓我把你吃了，
我才能為你說法。」

「如果你在說後面
那一半的偈頌之前就吃了我,
那我還是聽不到後面的偈頌,
這樣我死也不瞑目啊!
還是請先說給我聽,
然後再吃我吧!」

The *rakshasa* ghost glared at the Bhikshu with its big, red eyes.
"Oh! Do you want to hear more Buddhadharma?
But I am rather hungry, and I must eat something.
If I don't eat something,
I have no way to speak any more Buddhadharma!
Also, I love to eat human meat.
If you want me to speak more Dharma,
you will have to let me eat you."
"If you speak the last half of the verse after you eat me,
then I still won't hear it and then I won't die in peace.
How about this. Tell me the rest of it first, and then eat me!"

「好吧！下面兩句是這樣的：
『生滅滅已，寂滅為樂。』
我已經告訴你了，
哈！哈！現在準備當我的食物吧！」
「等一等，等一等！我要……」
這時比丘叫了起來，
羅剎鬼馬上喊著說：
「啊哈！我早就料到你一定會反悔的。」

"All right! The last two verses go like this:
'When production and extinction cease,
one reaches a state of serene quiescence.'
Now I have told you! Ha! Ha!
Get ready to become my food!"

"Wait, wait! I want to..."
the Bhikshu yelled.
The *rakshasa* immediately shouted,
"Aha!
I knew you would go back
on your promise."

「不！不是的。」
比丘急忙說：
「我只是想到如果我現在死了，
就再也沒有人可以聽見這句偈頌了！
所以讓我把這句偈頌刻在大樹幹上，
那麼以後無論誰經過這棵樹，
都可以讀到這首偈頌，
依法來修行。
等我把這偈頌刻好，
您就可以把我吃了。」
「喔！是嗎？好吧！
不要讓我等太久，
你趕快刻吧！」

"No, It's not that,"
The Bhikshu hurriedly said.
"I was just thinking that if I died,
no one would ever hear this verse!
So let me carve this verse
on the trunk of a big tree.
This way, in the future,
anyone who passes the tree can study these passages
and cultivate according to them.
Wait till I have carved these lines
before you eat me."
"Ho! Really?
All right then!
Don't make me wait too long;
hurry up and carve!"

這位比丘
把偈頌刻好後，
羅剎鬼就齜牙裂嘴，
撲向前去，
準備吃他的午餐時！
「等一等！」
「為什麼？你還想要求什麼？」
羅剎鬼不耐煩地吼叫起來。
「因為風雨會侵損樹幹的表皮，
那麼這些字便會磨滅了，
無法長久保存。
所以我想把它刻在石頭上，
才不會消失；
然後你就可以吃我了。」
比丘忙著說。
「好吧！」
羅剎鬼喃喃地抱怨說：
「你去刻吧！」

After the Bhikshu finished carving,

the *rakshasa* tightened his jaws and started to drool.

He was ready to eat.

"Wait!" said the Bhikshu.

"WHAT? What else do you want?"

the *rakshasa* ghost roared impatiently.

"Because the wind and rain

will wear away the words on the bark,

the verse won't keep long.

So let me carve these words in stone, and then you can eat me."

Annoyed, the *rakshasa* ghost said grumpily, "All right! Go carve it!"

於是，這位比丘就把偈頌刻到石頭上。刻好後，就盤起腿來，閉上眼睛，態度從容地等著羅剎鬼來吃他。

可是時間分分秒秒地過去了，四周靜悄悄地，什麼事也沒發生。當他睜開眼睛，卻發現羅剎鬼不見了！抬頭往空中一看，有個天人在那兒。原來這個鬼是天人變化來考驗他的！

After the Bhikshu carved the verse on a rock,

he closed his eyes, sat in full lotus,

and got ready for the ghost to eat him.

Time slowly ticked by,

and everything was very still.

Nothing happened.

When he opened his eyes, the *rakshasa* ghost was gone!

The Bhikshu glanced up and saw a heavenly being.

In reality, the *rakshasa* ghost was a heavenly being

who had come to test the Bhikshu.

「善哉！善哉！」天人說：
「為了求得兩句佛法，
您寧願捨棄自己的生命。
這才是真正的精進！」
　這就是釋迦牟尼佛
　　　在前生，
　為了半首偈頌
寧捨生命的故事。

The heavenly being said,
"Good indeed! Good indeed!
You were willing to give up your life for two lines
of the Buddhadharma.
This is true vigor!"
This was the past life of Shakyamuni Buddha
in which he was willing to give up his life
for the sake of two verses.

智慧出爐！
Your wisdom has surfaced!

請回答下列問題：
Let's see if you can answer the following questions:

- 什麼叫因地的修行？

What does cultivating at the level of planting causes mean?

- 羅剎鬼為什麼要吃這位比丘？

Why did the *rakshasa* ghost want to eat the Bhikshu?

- 這位比丘是怎麼樣的一位修行人？

What kind of cultivator was the Bhikshu?

- 你能背出這四句偈頌嗎？

Can you memorize the verse spoken by the *rakshasa* ghost?

布髮掩泥
Hair That Covered Mud

想不到這位老比丘
就是燃燈佛……
No one guessed that this Bhikshu
was Burning Lamp Buddha….

釋迦牟尼佛
往昔在因地時,
曾經是一位苦行者,
他專門修種種的苦行。
有一次,
他看到一個老比丘
從遠處走來,

In a former life,
Shakyamuni Buddha was a hermit
who specialized in various ascetic practices.
One time he saw an elderly Bhikshu
walking from afar.

可是前面的路上有很多泥水， 很難走。
於是他就躺到泥水裏，
等著老比丘走來時， 好從他身上走過去，
免得老比丘在泥水裏走， 弄髒了腳。

In front of him,

the road was covered with mud, which made it difficult to walk on.

Thus, the hermit lay in the mud

and waited for the elderly Bhikshu to come and walk over his body.

This would spare the elderly Bhikshu from walking

in the mud and dirtying his feet.

他躺到泥水裏後，
一看，哦！有幾尺的地方，
還有泥水，
於是把頭髮也打開來，
鋪在泥上，請這位老比丘
從上面走過去。

As he lay in the mud,
he looked around.
Oh no!
A portion of the ground was still uncovered.
So he spread out his hair to
cover the rest of the mud.
Then he invited the elderly Bhikshu to walk over it.

想不到
這位老比丘就是燃燈佛,
他隱藏佛的相好莊嚴,
而現出老比丘的樣子。

No one knew that
this elderly Bhikshu was Burning Lamp Buddha.
He had assumed the form of an elderly Bhikshu,
concealing the Buddha's adorned features.

燃燈佛從他身上走過去後，
就說：「善哉！善哉！
爾如是，吾亦如是。」
這就是讚歎他：
「你眞好啊！你眞好啊！
你是這樣子，我也是這樣子，
我們都是行人所不能行的行門。」
然後就為他授記：
「汝於來世，當得作佛，
號釋迦牟尼。」

After Burning Lamp Buddha walked over the hermit's body,

he said, "Good indeed! Good indeed!

You are like this; I am also like this."

What this praise meant was,

"You are very kindhearted! We are both very much alike.

We both would do what others wouldn't do."

Burning Lamp Buddha then made a prophecy,

"In the future, you will become a Buddha.

Your name will be Shakyamuni."

智慧出爐！
Your wisdom has surfaced!

請回答下列問題：
Let's see if you can answer the following questions:

- 為什麼苦行者要布髮掩泥？
Why did the hermit cover the mud with his own hair?

- 老比丘是誰？
苦行者又是誰的過去生？
Who was the elderly Bhikshu?
Who would the hermit become in the future?

法界佛教總會簡介

- 這是個一九五九年上宣下化老和尚在美國創辦的佛教團體。
- 我們的目的是要將佛教的真實義理，傳播於世界各地。
- 譯經、弘揚正法、提倡道德教育、利益一切眾生，這是我們的責任。
- 我們的宗旨：不爭、不貪、不求、不自私、不自利、不打妄語。
- 我們有萬佛聖城、法界聖城、金山聖寺、金聖寺、金輪聖寺、金佛聖寺等國際性道場二十多處。
- 我們有育良小學、培德中學、法界佛教大學、法界宗教研究院、國際譯經學院、僧伽居士訓練班等機構。
- 在這個團體的僧人都必須遵守佛制，日中一食，時刻穿著袈裟，也要持戒、念佛、參禪、研究教理，和合共住，獻身佛教。
- 歡迎你加入這個團體，讓我們朝著真、善、美的方向而行！

Brief Description of the Dharma Realm Buddhist Association

- The Dharma Realm Buddhist Association (DRBA) was established by Venerable Master Hua in 1959 in America.
- Its goal is to spread the true principles of Buddhism to all lands throughout the world.
- Translating the Buddhist canon, propagating the Proper Dharma, advocating ethics-based education, and benefiting all sentient beings are responsibilities we aim to fulfill.
- These are our guidelines: refrain from fighting, avoid being greedy, let go of seeking, transcend selfishness, stop looking for personal advantages, and say nothing that is not true.
- DRBA has more than twenty branches including the City of Ten Thousand Buddhas, the City of the Dharma Realm, Gold Mountain Monastery, Gold Wheel Monastery, Gold Buddha Monastery and other international monasteries.
- Our educational institutions include Instilling Goodness Elementary School, Developing Virtue Secondary School, Dharma Realm Buddhist University, the Institute for World Religions, International Translation Institute, and the Sangha and Laity Training Programs.
- The monastics in our Sangha strictly uphold the regulations of the Buddha, taking one meal a day at noon and wearing the precept sash at all times. We uphold the precepts, recite the Buddha's name, practice Chan meditation, study the teachings, reside together in harmony, and do our best to embody the Buddha's teachings.
- We welcome you to join us, to participate in our activities, and to progress with us along a path that emphasizes truth, goodness, and beauty.

宣化上人簡傳
A Brief Introduction to the Venerable Master Hsuan

來自白雪皚皚的中國東北長白山區。
十九歲出家修道，發願普渡一切眾生。
一九六二年將正確真實的佛法，
由東方帶到西方——美國。
創美國佛教史始有僧相之記錄——
一九六八年五位美國人在上人座下出家，
是在西方建立三寶的第一人。
建立美國第一座佛教大道場——萬佛聖城，
分支道場遍佈美加地區，乃至亞、澳。
一九九五年圓寂，「我從虛空來，回到虛空去」。
終其一生儘量幫助世界走向安樂光明的途徑，
大慈悲普渡，流血汗，不休息！

I vow to fully take upon myself all sufferings and hardships of all the living beings in the Dharma Realm.

願將法界所有一切眾生苦難，悉皆與我一人代受。

He came from the snow-laden vicinity of the Eternally White Mountains
in northeastern China.
At the age of nineteen, he became a Buddhist monk
and vowed to save all living beings.
In 1962 he brought the Proper Buddhadharma from East to West.
In 1968 five Americans took monastic vows under his guidance;
Thus he established the Sangha and the Triple Jewel on American soil.
He founded the City of Ten Thousand Buddhas,
the first large American Buddhist monastic community,
With affiliated branch monasteries in
the United States, Canada, Asia, and Australia.
In 1995 before he passed into stillness, he said,
"I came from empty space, and to empty space I will return."
Throughout his life he promoted peace and light in the world,
compassionately and tirelessly rescuing living beings.

Dharma Realm Buddhist Association Bhanch Monastery
法界佛教總會
分支道場
www.drba.org

法界佛教總會・萬佛聖城
Dharma Realm Buddhist Association &
The City of Ten Thousand Buddhas
P.O. Box 217 / 4951 Bodhi Way, Ukiah, CA 95482 U.S.A.
Tel: (707) 462-0939   Fax: (707) 462-0949

國際譯經學院 The International Translation Institute
1777 Murchison Drive, Burlingame, CA 94010-4504 U.S.A.
Tel: (650) 692-5912

法界宗教研究院（柏克萊寺）
Institute for World Religions (Berkeley Buddhist Monastery)
2304 McKinley Avenue, Berkeley, CA 94703 U.S.A.
Tel: (510) 848-3440

金山聖寺 Gold Mountain Monastery
800 Sacramento Street, San Francisco, CA 94108 U.S.A.
Tel: (415) 421-6117

金聖寺 Gold Sage Monastery
11455 Clayton Road, San Jose, CA 95127 U.S.A.
Tel: (408) 923-7243

法界聖城 City of the Dharma Realm
1029 West Capitol Avenue, West Sacramento, CA 95691 U.S.A.
Tel: (916) 374-8268

金輪聖寺 Gold Wheel Monastery
235 North Avenue 58, Los Angeles, CA 90042-4207 U.S.A.
Tel: (323) 258-6668

長堤聖寺 Long Beach Monastery
3361 East Ocean Boulevard, Long Beach, CA 90803 U.S.A.
Tel: (562) 438-8902

福祿壽聖寺 Blessings, Prosperity, and Longevity Monastery
4140 Long Beach Boulevard, Long Beach, CA 90807 U.S.A.
Tel: (562) 595-4966

華嚴精舍 Avatamsaka Vihara
9601 Seven Locks Road, Bethesda, MD 20817-9997 U.S.A.
Tel: (301) 469-8300

金峰聖寺 Gold Summit Monastery
233 First Avenue West, Seattle, WA 98119 U.S.A.
Tel: (206) 284-6690

金佛聖寺 Gold Buddha Monastery
248 E. 11th Avenue, Vancouver, B.C. V5T 2C3 Canada
Tel: (604) 709-0248

金法聖寺 Gold Dharma Monastery
3645 Florida Avenue, Kenner, LA 70065 U.S.A.
Tel: (504) 466-1626

華嚴聖寺 Avatamsaka Monastery
1009 Fourth Avenue S.W., Calgary, AB T2P 0K8 Canada
Tel: (403) 234-0644

美國法界佛教總會駐華辦事處（法界佛教印經會）
Dharma Realm Buddhist Books Distribution Society
台灣省台北市忠孝東路六段 85 號 11 樓
11th Floor, 85 Chung-Hsiao E. Road, Sec. 6, Taipei, R.O.C.
Tel: (02) 2786-3022, 2786-2474

法界聖寺 Dharma Realm Sagely Monastery
台灣省高雄縣六龜鄉興龍村東溪山莊 20 號
20, Tong-hsi Shan-chuang, Hsing-lung Village, Liu-Kuei,
Kaohsiung County, Taiwan, R.O.C.
Tel: (07) 689-3713

彌陀聖寺 Amitabha Monastery
台灣省花蓮縣壽豐鄉池南村四健會 7 號
7, Su-chien-hui, Chih-nan Village, Shou-Feng,
Hualien County, Taiwan, R.O.C.
Tel: (03) 865-1956

般若觀音聖寺（原紫雲洞 formerly Tze Yun Tung Temple）
Prajna Guan Yin Sagely Monastery
Batu 5 1/2, Jalan Sungai Besi, Salak Selatan,
57100 Kuala Lumpur, Malaysia
Tel: (03) 7982-6560

法界觀音聖寺（原登彼岸 formerly Deng Bi An）
Dharma Realm Guan Yin Sagely Monastery
161, Jalan Ampang, 50450 Kuala Lumpur, Malaysia
Tel: (03) 2164-8055

蓮華精舍 Lotus Vihara
136, Jalan Sekolah, 45600 Batang Berjuntai,
Selangor Darul Ehsan, Malaysia
Tel: (03) 3271-9439

法緣聖寺 Fa Yuan Sagely Monastery
1, Jalan Utama, Taman Serdang, Raya,
43300 Seri Kembangan, Selangor, Malaysia
Tel: (03) 8948-5688

馬來西亞法界佛教總會檳城分會
Malaysia Dharma Realm
Buddhist Association Penang Branch
32-32C, Jalan Tan Sri Ten Ewe Lim,
11600 Jelutong, Penang, Malaysia
Tel: (04) 281-7728

回向偈

願以此功德　莊嚴佛淨土
上報四重恩　下濟三塗苦
若有見聞者　悉發菩提心
盡此一報身　同生極樂國

Verse of Transference

May the merit and virtue accrued from this work
Adorn the Buddhas' Pure Lands,
Repaying the four kinds of kindness above
And aiding those suffering in the paths below.
May those who see and hear of this
All bring forth the resolve for Bodhi
And, when this retribution body is over,
Be born together in the Land of Ultimate Bliss.

The Rakshasa Ghost and the Bhikshu
羅剎鬼與比丘

國家圖書館出版品預行編目資料

羅剎鬼與比丘：佛陀過去生的故事＝Ghost and the Bhikshu: stories of the Buddha's past lives／宣化上人作；施菩提,葉麗珍插畫.――初版.――臺北市：法總中文部,2005〔民94〕

面： 公分

注音版
中英對照
ISBN 986-7328-00-0(平裝)
1.釋迦牟尼(Gautama, Buddha, 560-480 B.C.)—傳記

229.1　　　　　　　　　　　　93018620

作　者　宣化上人
插　畫　施菩提‧葉麗真

發行人　法界佛教總會‧佛經翻譯委員會‧法界佛教大學
　　　　The City of Ten Thousand Buddhas
　　　　P.O. Box 217
　　　　4951 Bodhi Way, Ukiah, CA 95482 U.S.A.
　　　　電話: (707) 462-0939　傳真: (707) 462-0949

　　　　The International Translation Institute
　　　　1777 Murchison Drive Burlingame,
　　　　CA 94010-4504 U.S.A.
　　　　Tel: (650) 692-5912　Fax: (650) 692-5056

出　版　法界佛教總會中文出版部
　　　　台灣省台北市忠孝東路六段 85 號 11 樓
　　　　電話: (02) 2786-3022, 2786-2474

出版日　西曆 2005 年 1 月 17 日‧初版一刷
　　　　佛曆 3032 年 12 月 8 日‧釋迦牟尼佛聖誕

Home page: www.drbachinese.org